Twelve thousand years ago, herds of American mastodons lived in southern New York's Hudson River Valley. This was during the ice age, when mile-high sheets of ice called glaciers buried the northern half of the state.

The mastodons were hairy, elephantlike animals similar to woolly mammoths. They were attracted to the lush vegetation in the Hudson Valley's wetlands. The mastodons fed on the spruce and pine trees in the postglacial forest.

Many mastodons got stuck in the valley's numerous peat bogs and died. Mastodons became extinct about ten thousand years ago, but some skeletons were preserved in the wet clay. The discovery of mastodon skeletons has enabled scientists to learn much about the animals. The very first skeleton was reassembled two hundred years ago, when no one knew what the animal was or when it had lived.

For David Macaulay

I would like to thank the following people for helping me with my research: Roy Goodman at the American Philosophical Society, Richard Babcock, Sidney Hart, Nathan, Mel Johnson, Anglea Degraw, Tom Kelleher, John Gramn, Dr. Gabriele Gruber, Frank Hasse, and the Smith Museum Village. I would also like to thank Dwight Warren for explaining the geologic past of Orange County, New York, and for inviting me to a dig for mastodon bones.

Walter Lorraine Books

www.houghtonmifflinbooks.com

Manufactured in China
SCP 10 9 8 7 6 5 4 3 2

Library of Congress Cataloging-in-Publication Data

Morrison, Taylor.
  [Great unknown]
  Mastodon mystery / Taylor Morrison.
    p. cm.
  Originally published: The great unknown. Boston : Houghton Mifflin, c2001.
  ISBN-13: 978-0-395-97494-0 (hardcover)
  ISBN-10: 0-395-97494-1 (hardcover)
  ISBN-13: 978-0-618-77130-1 (pbk.)
  ISBN-10: 0-618-77130-1 (pbk.)
  1. Mastodon—New York (State)—Newburgh—Juvenile literature. 2. Peale, Charles Willson, 1741–1827—Juvenile literature. 3. Paleontologists—United States—Biography—Juvenile literature. I. Title.
  QE882.P8M67 2006
  569'.67—dc22
                                        2006005867

MASTODON MYSTERY

Taylor Morrison

HOUGHTON MIFFLIN COMPANY BOSTON

Walter Lorraine Books

In the fall of 1799, a farmer named John Masten began to dig a manure pit on his land. It was common for farmers to dig up a gray clay called shell marl out of the Hudson Valley's peat bogs. They spread the marl on their fields to fertilize the crops.

The farmers dug through several feet of dark peat until they reached the thick gray marl underneath. One of the workers jammed his shovel into what he thought was a log. He quickly realized that it wasn't wood. It turned out to be the largest bone the men had ever seen.

Soon they were all digging wildly. Fueled by curiosity and grog, the farmers discovered many more bones embedded in the clay. To pull the biggest and heaviest ones out they used powerful teams of oxen. A big crowd gathered to see the bones of the mysterious beast. Unfortunately, before the farmers were able to unearth the entire skeleton, cold water from underground springs began to fill the pit. They could not continue the work.

Two years later, in 1801, Charles Willson Peale saw a newspaper clipping that described the discovery of giant bones in New York State. He was the creator of America's foremost natural history museum, in Philadelphia. Scientists around the world were puzzled by the bones.

The bones resembled those of an elephant. However, elephants live only in warm southern climates, so it didn't make sense that the bones had been found in North America. Similar bones had been turning up for nearly a century, but no one had ever seen the animal they belonged to. The discoveries of these bones were confusing to many, because people believed that God had created a perfect natural world and that he would not create an animal that would become extinct.

The most confusing part of the remains was the teeth, which were pointed, unlike the flat, ridged teeth of an elephant. The teeth led many people to believe that the animal was a fierce predator. Scientists could not identify the animal because no one had found enough bones to reconstruct a complete skeleton. They simply called it "The Great Unknown."

Peale was extremely excited after reading the article. He hoped to find a more complete skeleton in New York. That could solve the mystery and become the museum's greatest exhibit.

The next morning Peale departed from Philadelphia by stagecoach, headed
for New York City. There Peale boarded a Hudson River sloop and sailed north.
After three days of traveling, he reached Newburgh, New York.

Early the following morning Peale went to John Masten's farm. Masten had piled the bones on the floor of his granary, where he charged curious visitors to see them. The bones were battered and broken from the rough excavation, but it was the largest collection of such bones Peale had ever seen. He attempted to conceal his excitement and merely asked permission to make drawings of them. In the afternoon Peale was invited in for dinner. At the table, Masten's son demanded to know if he wished to buy the bones. Peale offered two hundred dollars for the bones and one hundred to dig up the rest of them. The Mastens argued that the price was too low, and they were unable to agree. After a long discussion Peale went back outside to work on his drawings.

The next day Masten accepted Peale's price, with a few additions. He also wanted gowns for his wife and daughters and a shotgun for his son. Peale was overjoyed. He packed up the bones and shipped them back to Philadelphia. There Peale planned an excavation to retrieve the rest of the skeleton. He received a five-hundred-dollar loan from the American Philosophical Society, which rented Peale its building for his museum. President Thomas Jefferson offered equipment from the army and navy to help with the dig. He shared Peale's enthusiasm about collecting the bones. Peale set off for New York with a small crew.

At Masten's farm, the pit where the bones had been dug up was full of water. Peale hired local craftsmen to build a giant pump.

Men walking on a treadmill caused a chain of buckets to rotate. The pump could remove 1,440 gallons of water an hour. The water was carried up to a long trough and from there into the fields. When the water level in the hole was low enough, the workers began digging, but soon water seeped back in and the soft walls of the pit began to crumble. Above, the tall timbers of the pump swayed in the wet ground. After digging for several days, Peale had to give up. The tired workmen were numb from the cold water. It was impossible to reach the rest of the bones under the soggy clay.

For the next two months Peale and his crew searched in other areas for the bones they needed to make a complete skeleton, particularly a lower jaw. Under the hot sun they drained and dug up several muddy bogs. After weeks of exhausting labor, they were rewarded with only a few decayed bones. At the third site, deep in a marshy forest, Peale was ready to give up the search. He was frustrated and running out of money to pay the workers.

Rembrandt, Peale's son, began probing the ground with a long iron spear. After trying many different places, he struck something hard. The crew began to dig at the spot and a bone slowly emerged. They shouted out cheers of joy when they unearthed a complete lower jaw. With renewed vigor, the mud-covered workers dug up a nearly complete skeleton. The next day they packed two wagons full of bones to send to Philadelphia.

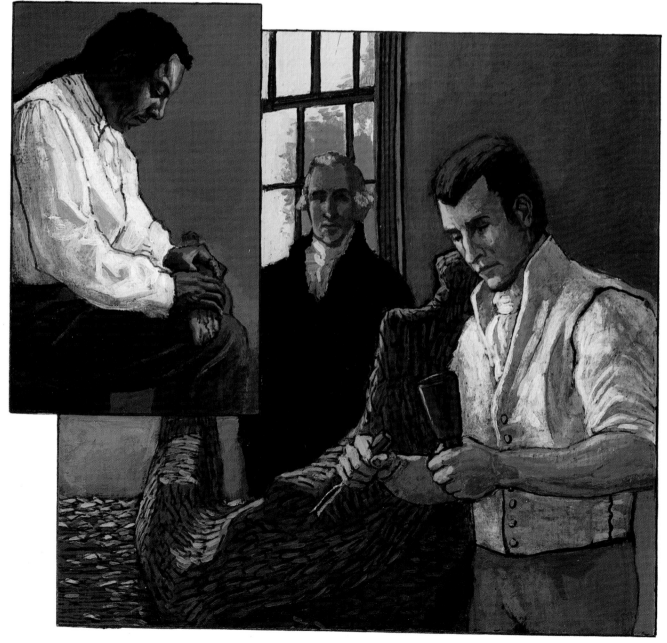

In the museum, mounting the skeleton was exciting but difficult work. There was no other skeleton in the world to which they could refer, and many of the bones were broken. Dr. Caspar Wistar, an expert on bones, helped Peale place them correctly. Rembrandt sketched out a plan to construct the skeleton. Moses Williams, Peale's assistant, figured out how many of the shattered pieces fit together.

Neither of the two skeletons was complete. They filled in the missing bones of one by referring to the skeleton of the other and by carving wooden replicas. Finally, the only major missing piece was the top of the head. Peale made a papier-mâché model of an elephant's skull and painted a red line between the real and the artificial bone.

Public excitement grew as the skeleton reached completion. It was finished after three months of work. People came to see it from all over the American colonies and the world. For an extra fifty cents one could enter the "Mammoth Room" in the museum.

Crowds of people gazed, and some even fainted before the monstrous skeleton. The skeleton helped to prove the argument that animals could become extinct. The bones existed, but the animals did not. In 1806, the French naturalist Georges Cuvier named the animal *mastodon,* which means "nipple tooth," because he thought its teeth resembled a woman's breasts. Thanks to Peale's efforts The Great Unknown was finally identified. Peale displayed the very first mastodon skeleton ever seen and only the second fossil skeleton known anywhere in the world.

In the late 1840s Peale's skeleton disappeared. Many believed it had been destroyed in a fire, but in 1953 the skeleton reappeared in Germany. It had been dismantled and secretly shipped to London. It eventually ended up in the natural history museum in Darmstadt, where it stands today. A great painting by Peale of the excavation hangs in the Maryland Historical Society.

For more detailed accounts of Peale's mastodon excavation, see the following books:

Miller, Lillian B., ed. *The Selected Papers of Charles Willson Peale and His Family*, vols. 1–4. New Haven: Yale University Press, 1983.

Peale, Rembrandt. *Historical Disquisition on the Mammoth; or, Great American Incognitum, an Extinct, Immense, Carnivorous Animal Whose Fossil Remains Have Been Found in North America.* London, 1803

Sellers, Charles Coleman. *Mr. Peale's Museum: Charles Willson Peale and the First Popular Museum of Natural Science and Art.* New York 1980.

Glossary

AMERICAN MASTODON (mass-toh-dahn): An animal very similar to an elephant. There were many different types of mastodons. They migrated to America about 15,000 years ago. Their remains have been found throughout the country but are most common in the Northeast.

AMERICAN PHILOSOPHICAL SOCIETY: Founded in 1743 by Benjamin Franklin, it was the first learned society in America. Its purpose was to promote useful knowledge. It was America's leading scientific institution at the time of Peale's excavation.

CUVIER, GEORGES: An expert on comparative anatomy in nineteenth-century France. He reconstructed many prehistoric animals from their fossilized bones.

FOSSIL: A remnant of a living thing from a prior geologic time.

GLACIERS: Massive sheets of compacted ice that have advanced and retreated in North America for about two million years.

GRANARY: A small, elevated outbuilding used by colonial farmers to store their grain.

GROG: A drink made of rum and water drunk by colonial workmen.

HUDSON RIVER SLOOP: A Dutch sailboat that transported passengers and goods up and down the Hudson River in the eighteenth and nineteenth centuries.

JEFFERSON, THOMAS: The third president of the United States. Jefferson helped to make natural history a respected and honorable pursuit. He loved natural history and even kept bones in the White House.

MAMMOTH: A long-haired, elephant-like animal that lived on the cold tundra close to the glaciers. The mammoths had a taller build than the mastodons, a high, domed head, and flat teeth, which they used to graze on grasses. At first the bones of mammoths discovered in Siberia were confused with those of the mastodon.

MARL: A type of clay used as fertilizer that preserves bones buried in it.

MASTEN, JOHN: A German-born farmer, probably descended from Palatine Germans, who settled Newburgh in 1709.

NEWBURGH: A town in Orange County, New York, that is famous for the large number of mastodon skeletons found there.

PAPIER-MÂCHÉ: The plastic of the nineteenth century. It is a mixture of paper pulp and glue used in molds to make forms and casts.

PEALE, CHARLES WILLSON: A soldier in the Revolutionary War, an artisan, a great portrait painter, and the founder of a natural history museum.

PEALE, REMBRANDT: One of Charles Willson Peale's many sons and an excellent portrait painter.

THE PEALE MUSEUM: In Peale's time, museums were only for kings, the wealthy, and scientists. His museum was the first of its kind, a place where the public was welcomed and encouraged to learn about nature.

PEAT BOG: A low-lying wet area that fills up with dead plant material called peat. The acidic peat prevents the decay of bones buried in it.

PHILOSOPHICAL HALL: The home of the Philosophical Society and of Peale's museum from 1794 to 1811.

POSTGLACIAL FOREST: A forest of evergreen trees that sprouted up from the tundra after the glaciers had retreated farther north.

WILLIAMS, MOSES: A former slave who worked for Peale in the museum. Williams was freed in 1803 and continued to work in Peale's museum, making silhouette portraits of visitors.

WISTAR, DR. CASPAR: President of the American Philosophical Society and the leading authority of the time on American fossils.